PIANO • VOCAL • CHORDS

Pop & Rock Hits
2008 Edition

Alfred Publishing Co., Inc.
16320 Roscoe Blvd., Suite 100
P.O. Box 10003
Van Nuys, CA 91410-0003
alfred.com

ISBN-10: 0-7390-5634-4
ISBN-13: 978-0-7390-5634-9

Cover photograph: Concert Crowd © istockphoto.com/dwphotos

CONTENTS

A-PUNK

Lyrics by
EZRA KOENIG

Music by
VAMPIRE WEEKEND

1. Jo -

-Punk - 5 - 1

%. *Verse:*

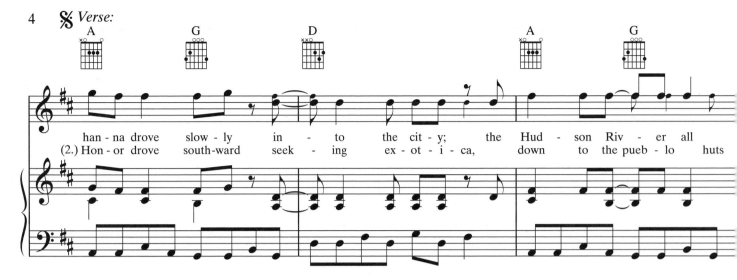

han - na drove slow - ly in - to the cit - y; the Hud - son Riv - er all
(2.) Hon - or drove south-ward seek - ing ex - ot - i - ca, down to the pueb - lo huts

filled with snow. She spied the ring___ on His Hon - or's fin - ger.
of New Mex - i - co. Cut his teeth___ on tur - quoise har - mon - i - cas.

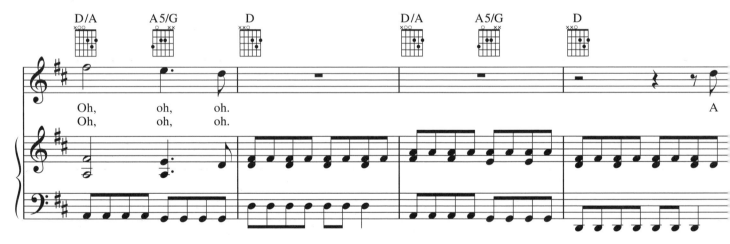

Oh, oh, oh.
Oh, oh, oh.

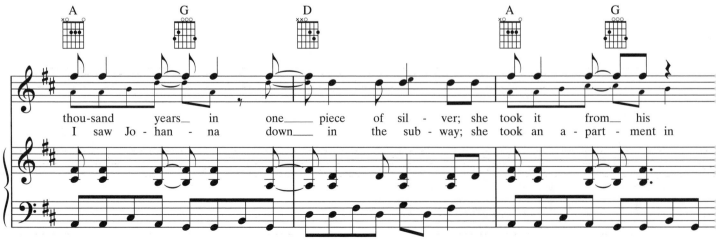

thou-sand years___ in one___ piece of sil - ver; she took it from___ his
I saw Jo - han - na down___ in the sub - way; she took an a - part - ment in

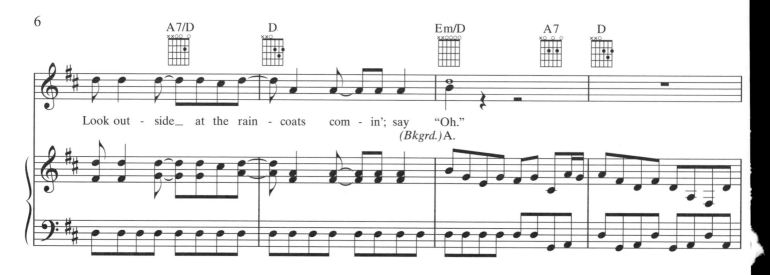

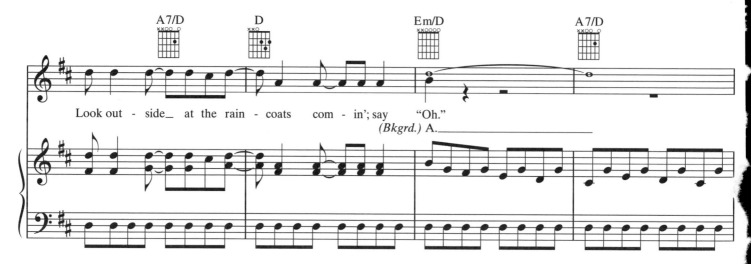

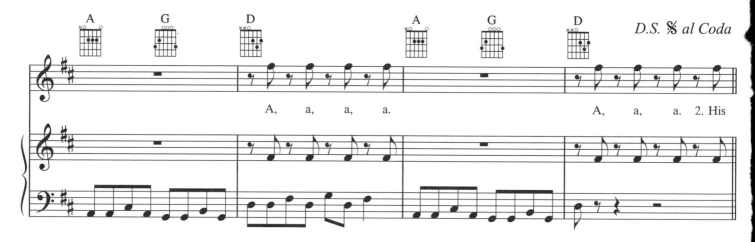

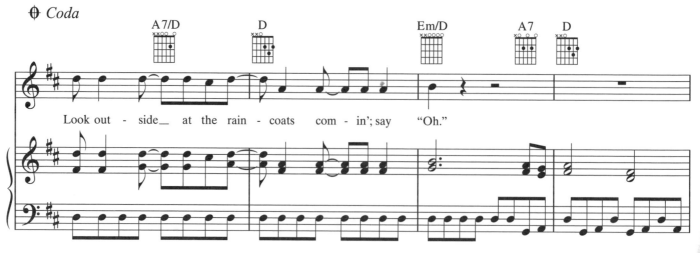

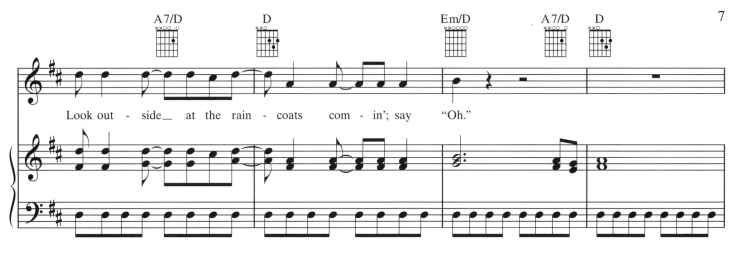

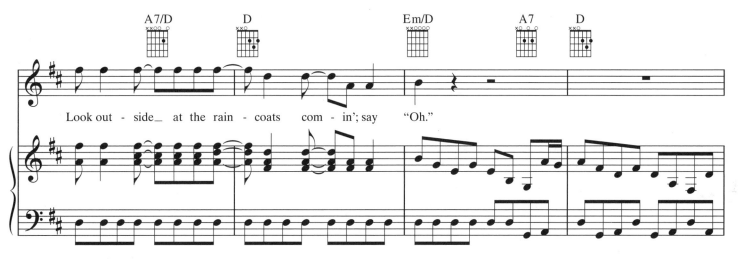

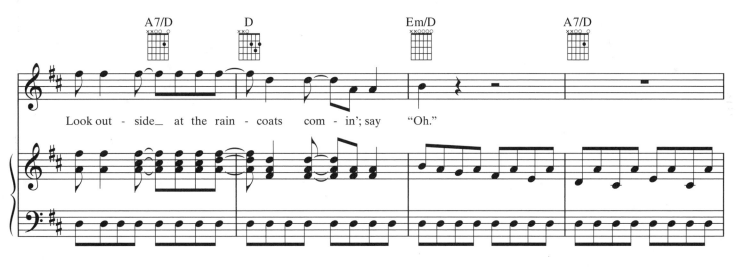

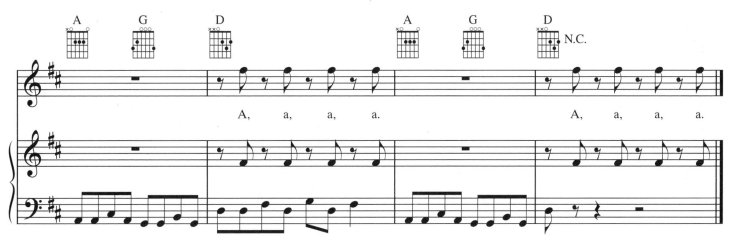

EVERYTHING

Words and Music by
MICHAEL BUBLÉ, ALAN CHANG
and AMY FOSTER-GILLIES

Chorus:

Chorus:

cra - zy life,_____ and through these cra - zy times,_

__ it's you,__ it's you.__ You make me sing.__ You're ev - 'ry line,_

__ you're ev-'ry word,_ you're ev-'ry - thing._____

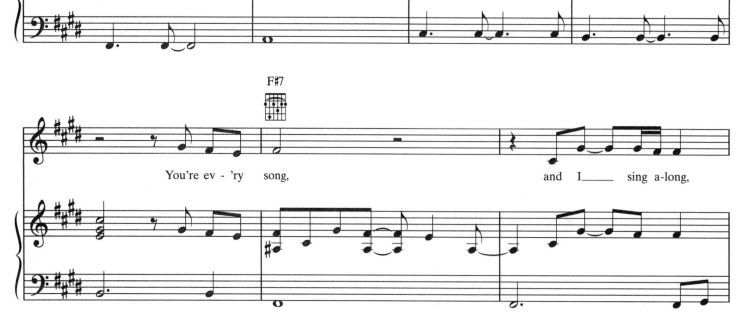

You're ev - 'ry song, and I__ sing a-long,

FALLING SLOWLY

Words and Music by
GLEN HANSARD and
MARKETA IRGLOVA

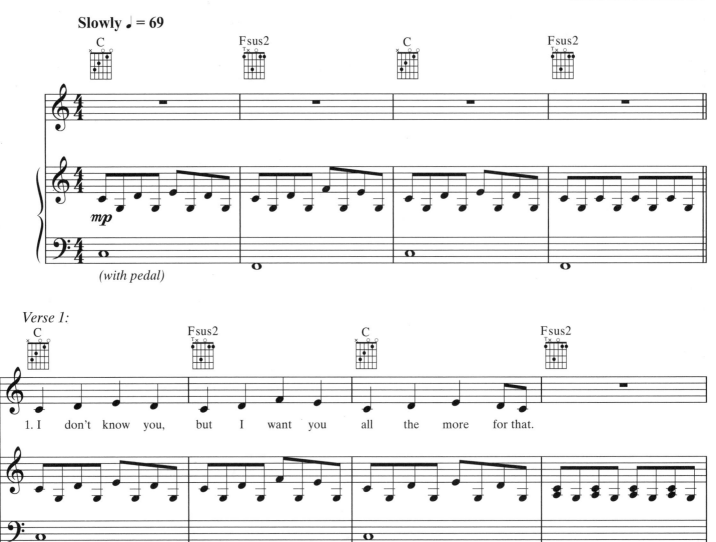

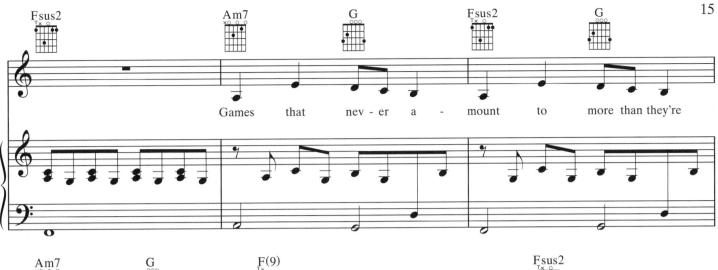

Games that nev - er a - mount to more than they're

meant will play them-selves out.

cresc.

Chorus:

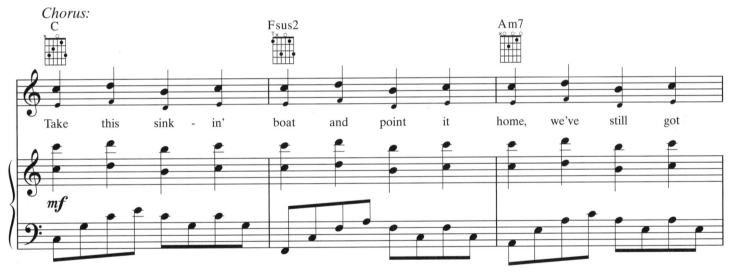

Take this sink - in' boat and point it home, we've still got

mf

time._____ Raise your hope - ful voice, you have a

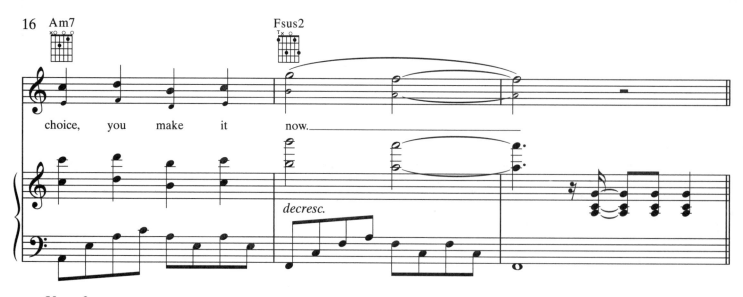

choice, you make it now._____

decresc.

Verse 2:

2. Fall - ing slow - ly, eyes that know me and I can't go back.

mp

Moods that take me and e - rase me and I'm paint - ed black.

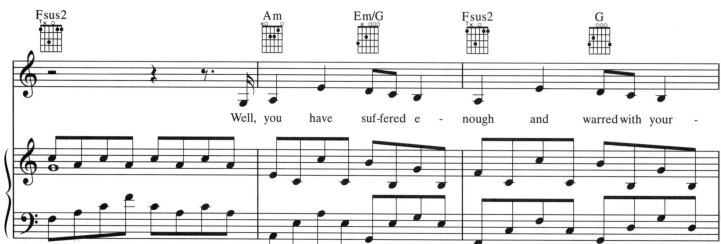

Well, you have suf-fered e - nough and warred with your -

Chorus:

(Strings)

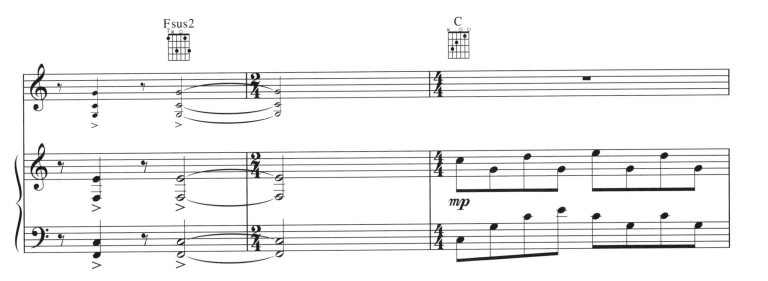

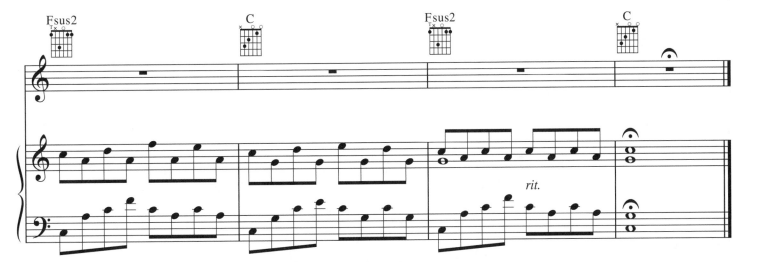

HEY THERE DELILAH

Words and Music by
TOM HIGGENSON

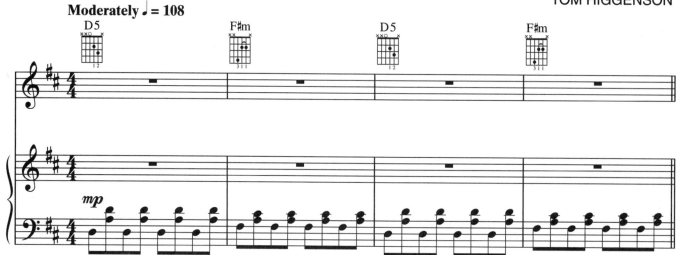

Verses 1 & 2:

1. Hey there, De - li - lah, what's_ it like in New_ York Cit - y? I'm a thou-
2. Hey there, De - li - lah, I_____ know times are get - ting hard, but just be - lieve_

sand miles a - way,_ but, girl,_ to - night_ you look so pret - ty, yes, you do.
_ me, girl, some-day_ I'll pay_ the bills_ with this gui - tar, we'll have it good.

Hey There Delilah - 7 - 1

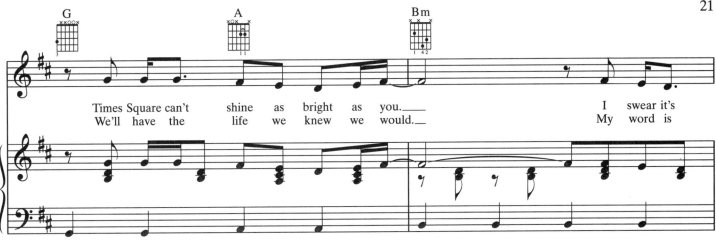

22

li - lah, I can prom-ise you__ that by__ the time__ we__ get through,__ the world__

__ will nev - er, ev - er be the same,_____ and you're to blame.__

Verse 3:

3. Hey there, De - li - lah, you be good__ and don't you miss__ me. Two more

26

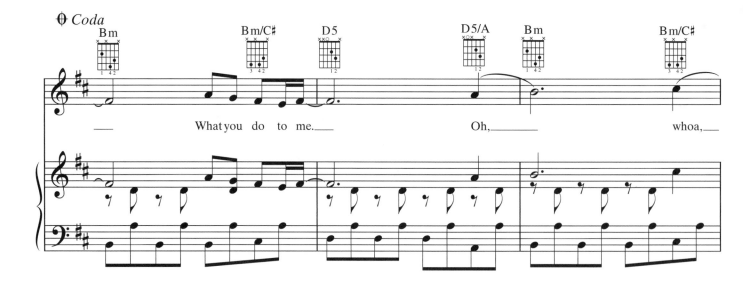

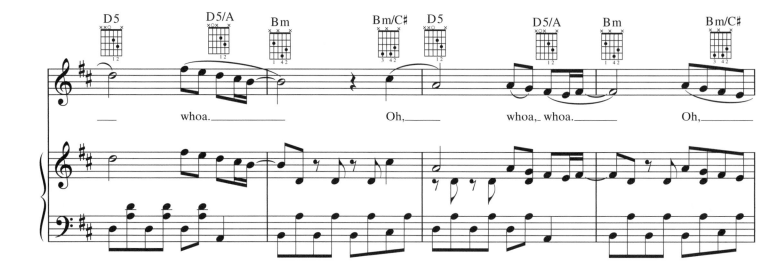

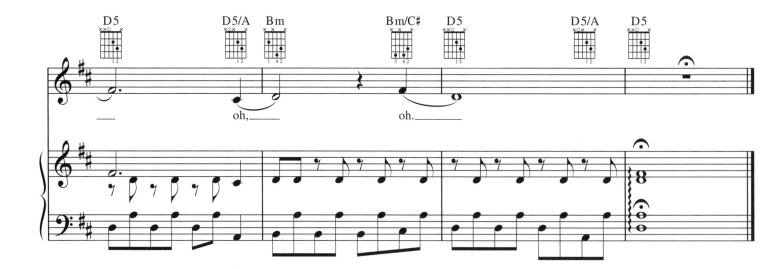

SORRY

Lyrics by
JOSH TODD and
MARTI FREDERIKSEN

Music by
JOSH TODD, KEITH NELSON
and MARTI FREDERIKSEN

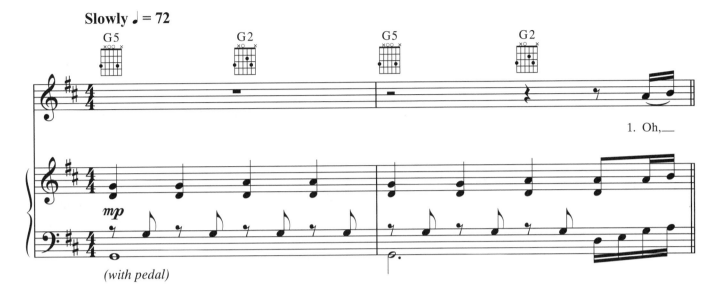

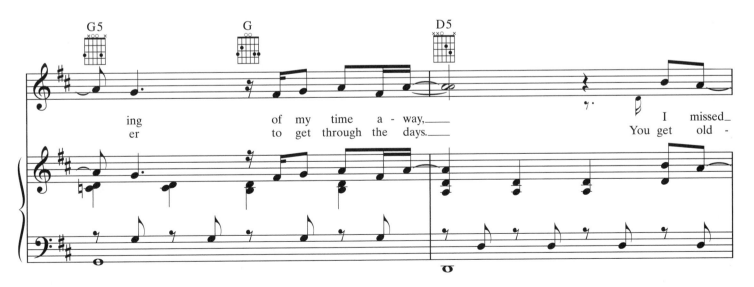

Bridge:

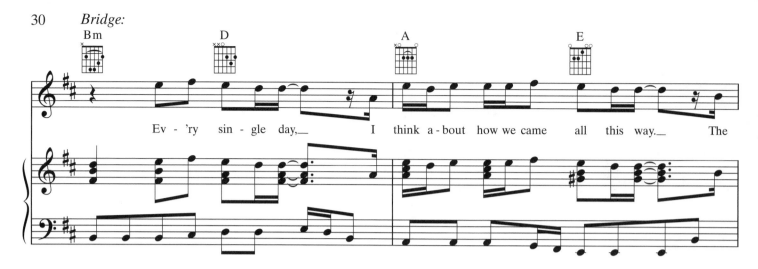

Ev - 'ry sin - gle day,_ I think a - bout how we came all this way._ The

sleep - less nights_ and the tears_ you cried,_ it's nev - er too late to make_

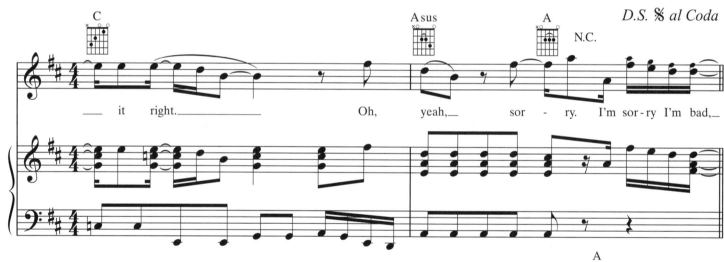

_ it right._ Oh, yeah,_ sor - ry. I'm sor - ry I'm bad,_

D.S. % al Coda

Coda

_ I'm sor - ry._

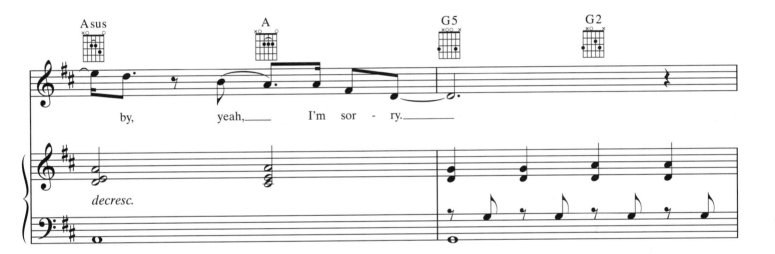

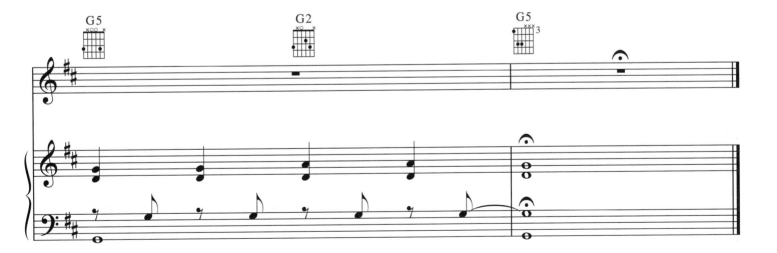

IN LOVE WITH A GIRL

Words and Music by
GAVIN DeGRAW

34

In Love With a Girl - 6 - 4

36

Chorus:

In Love With a Girl - 6 - 5

NEW SOUL

Words and Music by
YAEL NAIM and DAVID DONATIEN

Moderately ♩ = 100

Verses 1 & 2:

1. I'm a new soul, I came to this strange world hop - ing I could
young soul in this ver - y strange world, hop - ing I could

learn a bit 'bout how to give and take.__ But since I came here, felt the joy and
learn a bit 'bout what is true and fake.__ But why all this__ hate? Try to com - mu -

the fear, find - ing my - self mak - ing ev - 'ry pos - si - ble mis - take.__ }
ni - cate, find - ing trust and love is not al - ways eas - y to make.__ }

La la

New Soul - 6 - 2

42

A little slower

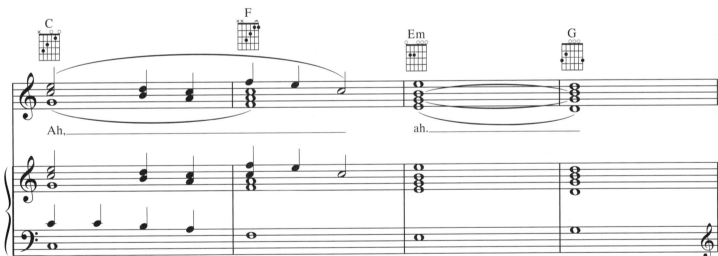

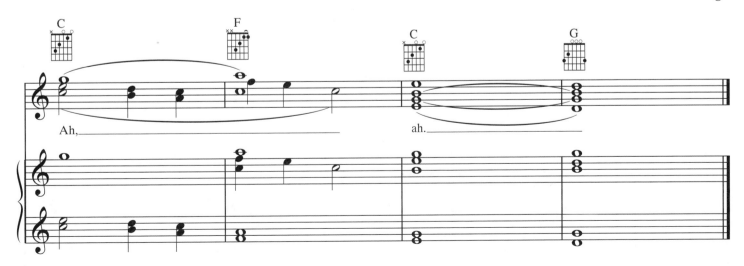

PRAYING FOR TIME

Words and Music by
GEORGE MICHAEL

Slowly ♩ = 69

1. These are the days of the o - pen hand._____ They will not be the
2. This is the year of the emp - ty hand._____ Oh, you hold on to what you

last. Look a - round, now.____ These are the days____ of the beg - gars and the choos-
can, and char - i - ty is a coat you wear____ twice a year.____

ers. This is the year of the hun - gry man,_____ whose place is in____ the
These are the days of the guilt - y man,_____ your tel - e - vi - sion takes a stand,_

Praying for Time - 4 - 1

46

and turned His back and all God's chil - dren crept__ out the back__
told you____ that He can't____ come back 'cause he has no chil - dren to come back__

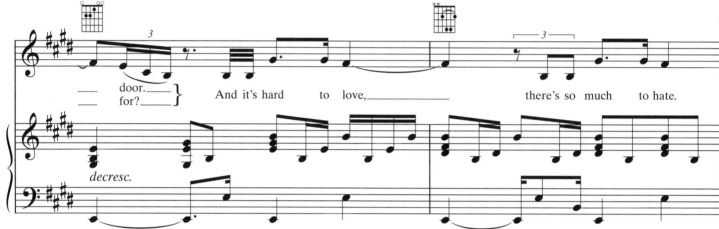

__ door.____
__ for?____ } And it's hard to love,_____ there's so much to hate.

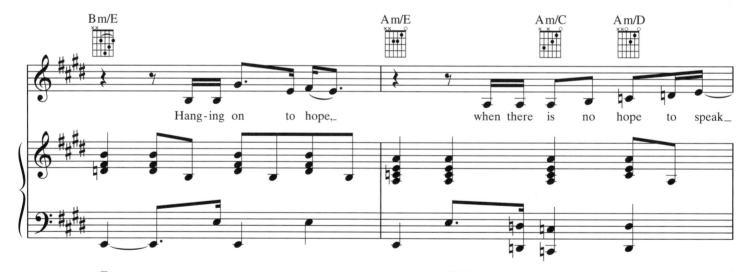

Hang-ing on to hope,__ when there is no hope to speak__

__ of. And the wound-ed skies a - bove____ say it's much too__

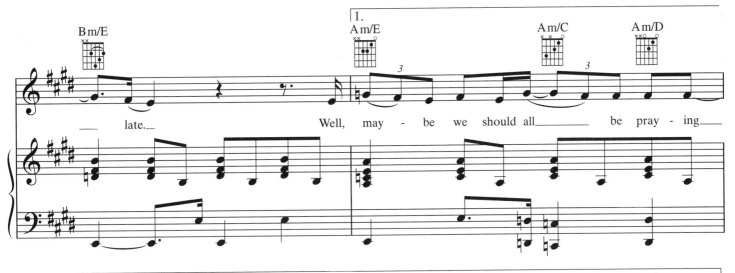

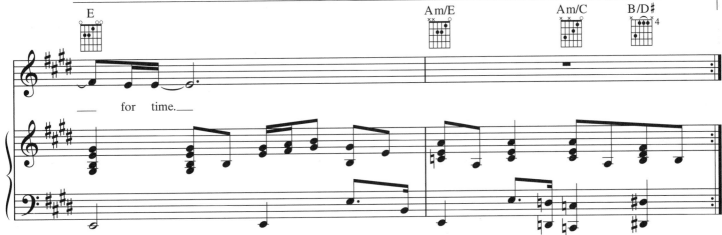

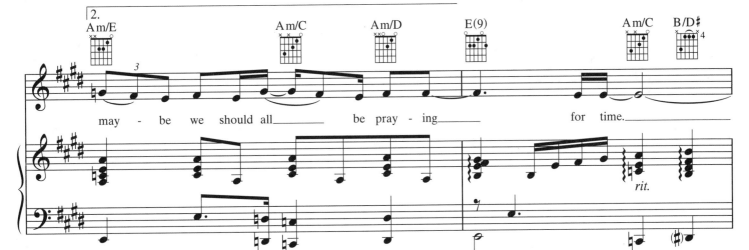

WHAT ABOUT NOW

Words and Music by
BEN MOODY, DAVID HODGES
and JOSH HARTZLER

Verses 2 & 3:

50

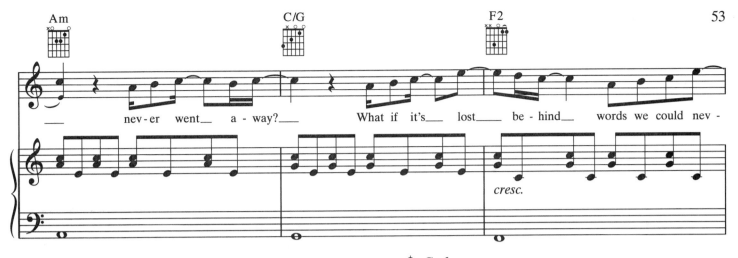

never went a-way?___ What if it's___ lost___ be-hind___ words we could nev-

cresc.

D.S. 𝄋 al Coda

⊕ Coda

er find?_ What a-bout_ now?_

Ba-by, be-fore___

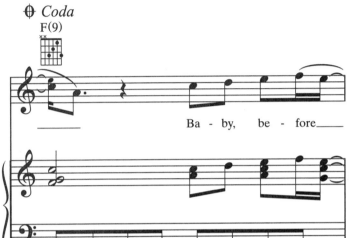

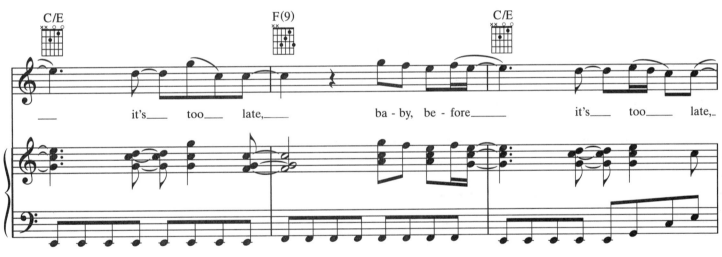

it's___ too___ late,___ ba-by, be-fore___ it's___ too___ late,_

what a-bout_ now?___

WHATEVER IT TAKES

Words and Music by
JASON WADE and JUDE COLE

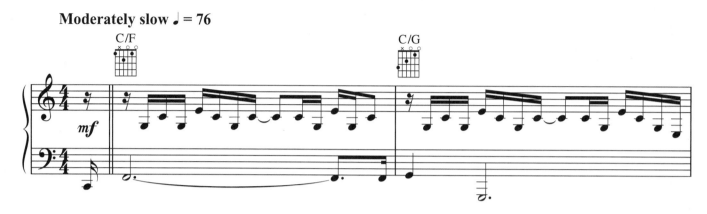

Chorus:

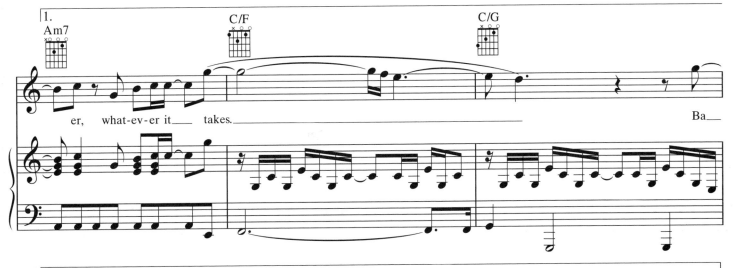

er, what-ev-er it___ takes._____ Ba__

__ ba ba ba ba._____ 2. She said,__

er. I know you de - serve___ much bet - ter. But re -

Bridge:

mem-ber the time I told you the way that I felt?____ That I'd__